CRIME WRITING 101

A Guide To Writing The Perfect Crime Novel

HACKNEY AND JONES

Copyright © 2023 by Hackney and Jones

All rights reserved.

No part of this book may be reproduced in any form or by any electronic or mechanical means, including information storage and retrieval systems, without written permission from the author, except for the use of brief quotations in a book review.

Contents

Also by Hackney and Jones	v
Introduction	vii
1. THE KEY ELEMENTS OF A CRIME NOVEL	1
Sub genres of crime fiction	2
2. HOW DO CRIME WRITERS MAKE MONEY?	4
Who is the wealthiest crime writer and how do they make money?	5
3. Quick Tips For Crime Writers Starting Out	6
4. Popular Crime Novels	8
5. Common Fears When Writing A Novel	11
6. Crime Writing Mistakes To Avoid	13
7. WHAT CRIME READERS DO AND DON'T WANT	15
What do crime readers want?	15
What don't they want?	17
8. CRIME WRITING CHECKLIST	18
Before writing	18
During writing	19
After writing	20
9. Researching The Legal System And Procedures	22
10. VIOLENCE IN CRIME NOVELS	24
The level of violence used in some common subgenres of crime fiction and why	25
11. Plotting or Pantsing?	27
12. Point Of View In Novel Writing	29
13. COMING UP WITH A CRIME IDEA FOR YOUR NOVEL	31
Some ideas for motives	31

14. PLOTTING AND STRUCTURING YOUR NOVEL	35
Your novel outline	36
Example of a basic novel outline you can use	37
15. Creating A Compelling Opening Scene	39
16. CREATING CHARACTERS	41
Creating a believable detective character	43
Creating a believable suspect character	44
Creating a full character profile	45
17. How To Incorporate Suspense In Your Crime Novel	47
18. How To Create A Sense Of Place And Atmosphere In Your Writing	49
19. Plot Twists	51
20. Red Herrings	54
21. Using Descriptive Language	56
22. WRITING DIALOGUE IN A CRIME NOVEL	58
Using different types of dialogue	59
Using dialogue to advance the plot	59
How to use dialogue in a novel with regards to gender	60
Dialogue in a novel with regards to pacing	62
Show not tell	63
23. HOW TO END YOUR NOVEL	65
Creating a satisfying and fitting ending for a novel	67
Using different types of endings	68
24. Crime Novel Book Titles	69
25. Crime Writing Word Count	71
26. CRIME FICTION BOOK COVER TIPS	73
Considerations when planning your crime novel book cover	75
27. Editors	76
28. Book Marketing	78
29. Crime Writing Glossary	80
Afterword	87

Also by Hackney and Jones

With **done-for-you templates** and step-by-step guidance, this workbook will take everything you've learned in Crime Writing 101 and help you turn it into a compelling and exciting crime novel.

Take the next step in your writing journey and order our companion workbook NOW!

Introduction

Welcome to **"Crime 101: A Guide To Writing The Perfect Crime Novel."**

This book is designed to provide you with all the tips and key elements you need to create a thrilling and engaging crime novel that will keep your readers on the edge of their seats. Inside, you will find everything from ideas for a crime novel, how to building the plot, crafting engaging characters, and mastering the art of dialogue.

We'll cover common mistakes to avoid, important research to conduct, and how to create a captivating opening scene. You'll learn about the importance of plot twists, red herrings, and endings that will leave your readers guessing until the very end. We'll also delve into the world of marketing, book covers, and writing from different points of view.

We created this book because we want to give you the straight-forward answers to all the most common questions around crime writing.

We've learned some of these lessons the hard way and we don't want you to have to go through the same. This book is the foundation of knowledge that will set you up for success in your novel writing career.

By reading this book (or any of our other books), you will have the confidence and knowledge to take action and create amazing novels that your readers will love and that will earn you money.

Reading this will give you the best possible start in your writing journey, so that you can write with confidence and create amazing novels that your readers will love and you will be proud of!

It is purposely designed to be a **zero-fluff** blue-print with **actionable tips** that you can easily reference from.

We don't want you to wade through mud finding the important bits, we give them to you on a plate.

This guide will help you turn your crime novel into a bestseller. So, if you're ready to take the first step in becoming a successful crime novelist, let's dive in!

The Key Elements Of A Crime Novel

Crime fiction is a genre of fiction that focuses on criminal activity and the investigation, prosecution, and punishment of criminals.

It can include novels, short stories, and plays, and can encompass a wide range of sub genres, such as detective fiction, mystery fiction, and thriller fiction.

Some of the key elements of crime fiction include a crime, usually murder, that is committed; a detective or other law enforcement figure who is tasked with solving the crime; and a sense of suspense and tension as the story unfolds.

Crime fiction is one of the most popular and enduring genres of literature, with many classic and contemporary works that continue to captivate readers and inspire new writers.

The key elements of a crime novel include:

Crime: The novel centres around a criminal act, such as a murder, theft, or fraud. This crime sets the plot in motion and drives the story forward.

Detective or investigator: This character is responsible for solving the crime and bringing the perpetrator to justice. They may be a professional detective, a private investigator, or an amateur sleuth. Examples include Sherlock Holmes, Hercule Poirot, and Kinsey Millhone.

Suspects: These are the characters who are believed to have committed the crime. They may be portrayed sympathetically or as obvious villains. The detective or investigator must sift through the evidence and interview the suspects to determine the true culprit.

Resolution: The crime is solved and the perpetrator is brought to justice in the end. This conclusion may be sudden and surprising, or it may be the result of a gradual uncovering of the truth.

Setting: The story usually takes place in a specific location which is often a city or small town, with a sense of atmosphere and mood that enhances the story.

Motive: The reason for the crime is often revealed and motives can be complex and varied. It could be money, revenge, love, or power.

Tension and suspense: Crime novels are often characterised by an atmosphere of tension and suspense, as the reader is kept guessing about the outcome of the story, who the criminal is, and how the crime will be solved.

Sub genres of crime fiction

There are many sub genres of crime fiction, each with their own unique characteristics and themes.

Some of the most popular sub genres include:

Noir fiction: Noir fiction is characterised by its dark, gritty, and often cynical tone. It typically features hard-boiled detectives, femme fatales, and corrupt characters. Noir fiction often explores themes of crime, corruption, and moral ambiguity.

Noir historical fiction: Noir historical fiction combines Noir fiction with a historical setting and often includes a historical crime or mystery. They often feature a detective or a criminal trying to solve a crime in a historical context.

Cozy mystery: Cozy mysteries are characterised by their light tone, gentle humour, and a focus on amateur detectives. They typically take place in small towns or villages and feature a closed group of suspects. They usually feature no graphic violence or sex.

Police procedural: Police procedural novels focus on the process of solving a crime, usually through the eyes of the police detectives. They often provide a detailed and realistic portrayal of police procedures and forensic science.

Legal thriller: Legal thrillers focus on legal procedures and court cases, often with an emphasis on the legal system and the motivations of the characters. They often involve legal battles, trials, and appeals.

Psychological crime fiction: Psychological crime fiction explores the psychological motivations of the characters and the criminal mind. They often focus on the psychological process of solving a crime, rather than the physical evidence.

True crime: True crime novels are based on real-life criminal cases and often include in-depth research and interviews with those involved in the case. They usually focus on the investigation and prosecution of a specific crime.

2

How Do Crime Writers Make Money?

Crime writers make money through a variety of channels, including:

Book sales: The most common way for crime writers to make money is through book sales. They can earn royalties from the sale of their books, both in print and digital formats.

Advances: Many crime writers receive advances from publishers for their work. An advance is a sum of money paid to the author before the book is published, and is typically based on the publisher's estimate of the book's future sales.

Film and TV adaptations: Crime writers can also make money from the sale of rights for film and TV adaptations of their books.

Speaking engagements: Some crime writers also make money from speaking engagements, such as book signings, conferences, and other events.

Merchandising: Some crime writers also make money from

merchandising, such as book-related merchandise like mugs, t-shirts, and other items.

Who is the wealthiest crime writer and how do they make money?

The wealthiest crime writer is James Patterson. He is known for his bestselling series featuring characters such as Alex Cross, Michael Bennett, and Women's Murder Club. He has sold over 300 million copies of his books worldwide and has had many of his books adapted into movies and TV shows.

He makes money through book sales, advances, film and TV adaptations, and merchandising. Patterson is also known for co-authoring books with other writers, which also adds to his income.

3

Quick Tips For Crime Writers Starting Out

Read widely in the genre: Read as much crime fiction as you can to get a sense of the different styles, sub genres, and conventions of the genre.
Reading different authors, styles, and sub genres will also give you an idea of what you like and don't like as a writer and reader.

Study the basics of storytelling: Understand the basic principles of storytelling, such as plot, character, dialogue, and setting. Understanding these elements will help you create a compelling and well-structured story.

Create a strong and believable protagonist: The protagonist is the character who the readers will follow throughout the story, so make sure the protagonist is relatable and interesting.

Create a compelling villain: The villain is often the driving force behind the story, so make sure the villain is believable, interesting, and has a clear motivation.

Research the criminal justice system: It's important to understand the real-world mechanics of the criminal justice system, including the legal process, police procedures, and forensic techniques.

Pay attention to detail: Crime fiction often requires a lot of research, pay attention to the details of your story, including the setting, characters, and the crime itself.

Create tension and suspense: Crime fiction is often driven by tension and suspense, make sure to create a sense of urgency and unease throughout your story, so that readers will be drawn in and kept on the edge of their seats.

Write what you know: Write about things you know and understand well, it will make your writing more authentic and believable.

Get feedback and revise: Share your writing with beta readers, get feedback and revise your work to make it the best it can be.

Never stop learning and growing: Writing is a craft that takes time and practice to master, continue to learn and grow as a writer by attending workshops, writing groups, and reading books on writing.

Remember that writing a crime novel can be a challenging, but it's also a very rewarding experience, and with practice, perseverance and patience, you can hone your writing skills and create a great crime fiction novel that readers will enjoy.

4

Popular Crime Novels

Here are some of the most popular crime fiction novels that may be helpful for a beginner crime writer to read:

"The Girl with the Dragon Tattoo" by Stieg Larsson - A gripping thriller that delves into the dark underbelly of a wealthy Swedish family and the secrets they try to hide.

"The Silence of the Lambs" by Thomas Harris - A classic psychological thriller that follows an FBI agent as she tracks down a serial killer.

"Kiss the Girls" by James Patterson - A fast-paced thriller that follows a detective as he races against time to track down a serial kidnapper.

"Gone Girl" by Gillian Flynn - A dark and twisty thriller that explores the marriage of a couple and the mystery surrounding the wife's disappearance.

"The Lincoln Rhyme series" by Jeffery Deaver - A series of crime novels that follow the investigations of quadriplegic detective

Lincoln Rhyme, who uses his intellect and state-of-the-art technology to solve crimes.

"The Harry Hole series" by Jo Nesbo - A series of crime novels that follow the investigations of detective Harry Hole, who is known for his unorthodox methods and complex personal life.

"The Girl on the Train" by Paula Hawkins - A psychological thriller that tells the story of a divorcee who becomes embroiled in a missing persons case involving her ex-husband and his new family.

"The Cuckoo's Calling" by Robert Galbraith (J.K. Rowling) - A detective novel that follows private investigator Cormoran Strike as he investigates the death of a model, that at first glance seemed like a suicide

"The Inspector Gamache series" by Louise Penny - A series of crime novels that follow the investigations of Chief Inspector Armand Gamache, who leads the homicide department of the Sûreté du Québec.

"The Inspector Montalbano series" by Andrea Camilleri - A series of crime novels that follow the investigations of Inspector Salvo Montalbano, who works in the Sicilian town of Vigata.

"The Inspector Lynley series" by Elizabeth George - A series of crime novels that follow the investigations of Detective Inspector Thomas Lynley, who is a member of Scotland Yard's elite murder squad.

"The Inspector Morse series" by Colin Dexter - A series of crime novels that follow the investigations of Inspector Endeavour Morse, who is a detective with the Oxford City Police.

"The Inspector Banks series" by Peter Robinson - A series of crime novels that follow the investigations of Detective Chief Inspector Alan Banks, who works for the Eastvale Police in the UK.

"The Black Echo" by Michael Connelly - The first book in the Harry Bosch series, it follows the investigations of LAPD detective Harry Bosch, who is tasked with solving the murder of a fellow Vietnam veteran. The book is a great example of a detective novel, showcasing the main character's dedication and persistence in solving the crime, as well as the complexity of the case and the character of Harry Bosch himself.

Common Fears When Writing A Novel

Here is a breakdown of the most common rears when writing a novel:

Fear of not being good enough: Many writers worry that their writing is not good enough to be published, or that they will be criticised for their work. To overcome this fear, it's important to remember that every writer starts somewhere, and that practice and persistence are key to improving your writing. Try to find a writing group or workshop to get feedback from other writers, and be open to constructive criticism. Also, read and study the works of successful authors to gain inspiration and understanding of the craft.

Fear of writer's block: Writer's block is a common fear among writers, and it can be caused by a variety of factors, including stress, lack of inspiration, and self-doubt. To overcome writer's block, try to identify the root cause of the problem and address it. For example, if stress is causing the block, try to find ways to relax and reduce stress. If you're struggling to come up with ideas, try brainstorming or free-writing.

Fear of rejection: Many writers fear rejection from agents or publishers, and this fear can be debilitating. To overcome this fear, it's important to remember that rejection is a normal part of the writing process. Even the most successful authors have been rejected many times before getting published. Try to view rejection as an opportunity to learn and improve, and don't take it personally.

Fear of not finishing: Some writers fear that they will not be able to finish their novel. To overcome this fear, it's important to set realistic goals for yourself, and break the novel down into manageable chunks. Also, try to find an accountability partner to keep you on track.

Fear of criticism: Some writers fear that their work will be criticised or not well received by readers. To overcome this fear, remember that not everyone will like your work and that's okay. Keep in mind that you wrote the book for yourself, not for others. Also, try to separate yourself from your work, and don't take criticism personally.

In general, to overcome these fears, it's important to remember that writing is a process, and that improvement takes time and effort. Stay positive, stay motivated, and don't give up on your writing goals.

6

Crime Writing Mistakes To Avoid

Below are some of the most common writing mistakes to try and avoid in your crime writing:

- Using too much jargon or technical language that is not well-explained.
- Failing to conduct proper research on criminal procedures, forensic science, and other relevant details.
- Creating unrealistic or inconsistent character motivations or behaviours.
- Ignoring or glossing over the effects of trauma on victims and witnesses.
- Relying on stereotypes or clichés in character development and plot.
- Neglecting to show the consequences of criminal actions on both the perpetrator and the community.
- Not having a clear understanding of the legal system and the roles of different law enforcement agencies.
- Failing to create a believable and compelling plot that keeps readers engaged.
- Not showing the emotional and psychological aspects of the crime and its investigation.

- Focusing too much on violence and gore rather than the motives and emotions behind the crime.
- Neglecting to show the perspectives of different characters, especially those from marginalised communities.
- Not accurately depicting the cultural and societal context in which the crime takes place.
- Failing to create a sense of tension and suspense throughout the story.
- Not providing enough detail or explanation for forensic evidence or other technical aspects.
- Including too many subplots or characters, making the story feel convoluted and hard to follow.
- Not showing the impact of the crime on the community and the victims' loved ones.
- Focusing too much on the detective or investigator's personal life, taking away from the crime story.
- Not including enough twists and turns in the plot to keep readers guessing.
- Depicting law enforcement or the legal system in an overly positive or negative light without nuance.
- Not providing a satisfying resolution or conclusion to the story.

7

What Crime Readers Do And Don't Want

What do crime readers want?

Crime readers typically look for a few key elements in a crime novel.

They want:

Suspense and tension: Crime readers want to be on the edge of their seats, wondering what will happen next. They want to be kept in suspense and be surprised by the outcome.

Sense of danger and excitement: Crime readers enjoy danger and excitement, whether it's the danger of the crime itself or the risk and danger faced by the characters as they try to solve the crime.

Intellectual stimulation: Crime fiction often requires readers to think critically and pay attention to details as they try to solve the crime along with the characters.

Exploration of human nature: Crime readers enjoy the darker aspects of human nature, such as greed, jealousy, and obsession, which can be fascinating and thought-provoking.

Complexity and depth: Crime readers enjoy complex and morally ambiguous issues, which can make for a more engaging and satisfying reading experience.

Escapism: Crime readers want to escape into a different world and experience the thrill of a crime being solved, so that they can forget their own problems and be fully immersed in the story.

A compelling plot: Crime readers want a story that is fast-paced, suspenseful, and filled with twists and turns. They want to be kept guessing until the end, and be surprised by the outcome.

Engaging characters: Crime readers want to connect with the characters in the story. They want to understand the motivations, backgrounds, and personalities of the characters, and see how they react to the crime and the investigation.

Authenticity: Crime readers want the story to be believable and authentic. They want the story to be grounded in reality, and for the crime, the investigation, and the resolution to be realistic.

A sense of justice: Crime readers want to see the perpetrator of the crime brought to justice, whether by the police, the detective, or the victim. They want to see that the criminal is punished for their actions.

A well-written prose: Crime readers want to read a well-written and enjoyable prose, they want to be taken on a journey and be transported to the world of the story, they want to be engaged by the writing style.

By including these elements in a crime novel, an author can create a story that appeals to crime readers and keeps them engaged from start to finish.

What don't they want?

Crime readers typically do not want certain elements in a crime novel.

They don't want:

Predictable plots: Crime readers want a story that is full of twists and turns, they don't want to be able to predict the outcome. If the story is too predictable, it can become boring and fail to hold their interest.

Flat or uninteresting characters: Crime readers want to connect with the characters in the story, if the characters are uninteresting or flat, it can be hard for the readers to care about the story and the outcome.

Inaccurate or unrealistic depictions of crime and investigation: Crime readers want the story to be authentic, if the story is full of inaccuracies or unrealistic depiction of crime and investigation, it can break their suspension of disbelief and make it hard for them to engage with the story.

Lack of tension: Crime readers want to be on the edge of their seats, if the story lacks tension and suspense, it can become uninteresting and fail to hold their attention.

Unsatisfying ending: Crime readers want to see justice done, they want a sense of closure, if the ending is not satisfying and leaves loose ends, it can be frustrating and fail to meet their expectations.

Poorly written prose: Crime readers want to read a well-written and enjoyable prose, if the writing is poor, it can be hard for them to engage with the story and become invested in the characters and the plot.

8

Crime Writing Checklist

Before writing

Research the crime genre and read successful crime novels to gain inspiration and understand conventions.
Examples: "The Girl with the Dragon Tattoo" by Stieg Larsson, "Kiss the Girls" by James Patterson, "The Silence of the Lambs" by Thomas Harris.

Develop a detailed outline of the plot, including the crime, suspects, and resolution.
Examples: Create a plot summary, create a character map, create a timeline of events.

Create complex, realistic characters with distinct motivations and backgrounds.
Examples: Create detailed character profiles, conduct interviews with your characters, create a backstory for each character.

Research the setting and create a believable and immersive environment.

Examples: Visit the location, conduct online research, read books or articles on the location.

Familiarise yourself with legal procedures and forensic techniques that will be featured in the novel.
Examples: Read books or articles on forensic science, criminal psychology, and crime scene investigation, talk to experts in the field, watch shows or movies that feature the same subject matter.

During writing

Write a detailed and engaging opening chapter that sets the scene and grabs the reader's attention. **Examples:** Start with a crime or an intriguing question, include vivid descriptions of setting and characters, include a hook or a cliff-hanger.

Follow the three-act structure:

Act 1: Introduce the characters, setting, and the crime. Establish the main conflict and the stakes.

Act 2: Develop the plot by introducing new characters, clues, and obstacles. Raise the tension and create a sense of urgency.

Act 3: Reach the climax, reveal the perpetrator and the resolution. Tie up loose ends and provide a satisfying ending.

Divide the story into chapters and ensure that each chapter serves a purpose.
Examples: Each chapter should advance the plot, reveal something new about the characters or the setting, or increase the tension.

Keep the plot moving by adding twists and turns and building tension.

Examples: Introduce new characters and information gradually, use foreshadowing and red herrings, create a sense of urgency.

Show, don't tell, by using descriptive language and action to reveal character traits and advance the plot.
Examples: Use dialogue to reveal character's personalities, use sensory details to create a sense of atmosphere and mood, use body language and actions to reveal emotions.

Continuously revise and edit the manuscript to ensure that it is polished and free of errors.
Examples: Read your manuscript aloud, have beta readers give feedback, use editing software or online tools.

Take regular breaks to avoid burnout and to come back to the manuscript with fresh eyes.
Examples: Take a walk, exercise, read a book, spend time with family and friends.

After writing

Seek feedback from beta readers and incorporate their suggestions.
Examples: Share the manuscript with a small group of readers you trust, consider feedback from other writers, ask for specific feedback on plot, characters, pacing and dialogue.

Revise the manuscript one final time, addressing any remaining plot holes or inconsistencies.
Examples: Check for consistency in characterisations, pacing and plot, check for errors in grammar and punctuation, check for continuity errors.

Research potential agents or publishers, and tailor your query letter and synopsis to their preferences.
Examples: Look for agents or publishers who specialise in crime

fiction, read their guidelines and submission requirements carefully, tailor your query letter and synopsis to their preferences.

Prepare a marketing plan, including social media and events to promote the book.
Examples: Create a website, author page, and blog to promote your book, plan a book launch event and book signings, use social media to connect with readers and other writers.

Self-publish or traditionally publish the book and continue to market and promote it.
Examples: Keep promoting the book even after its release by doing interviews, writing articles and participating in literary events, use online platforms to reach a larger audience, consider audiobook and eBook versions.

9

Researching The Legal System And Procedures

Researching the legal system and procedures for your crime novel is an important aspect of making your story believable and accurate.

Additionally, consulting with experts in fields related to the investigation, such as law enforcement or forensic scientists, can provide valuable insight and help add credibility to the story.

Incorporating realistic details and avoiding common clichés or inaccuracies in the portrayal of the investigation can also add to the believability of the story. It is also important to consider the motivations and backgrounds of the characters involved in the investigation, as well as the potential suspects and their alibis.

Here are some actionable steps you can take to research the legal system and procedures for your crime novel:

Consult legal textbooks: Legal textbooks can provide a wealth of information on the legal system and procedures. They can give you an overview of the laws, the court system, and the different types of cases that are heard in court. Many universities and law schools have libraries that are open to the public, where you can access legal textbooks.

Speak to legal professionals: Legal professionals such as lawyers, judges, and prosecutors have a wealth of knowledge and experience in the legal system. They can provide you with information on how the legal system works, the procedures that are followed in court, and the challenges that legal professionals face. You can reach out to them for interviews or even job shadowing.

Observe court proceedings: Observing court proceedings can give you a firsthand look at how the legal system works. You can observe the proceedings from the public gallery and take note of the different stages of the trial and the roles of the different participants, such as the judge, the lawyers, and the witnesses.

Research online and watch legal dramas: There are a lot of resources online that can help you research the legal system and procedures. There are websites and blogs that provide information on the legal system and court procedures, as well as legal dramas on television and streaming services that can give you an idea of how the legal system works in the context of a crime story.

Join legal organisations and attend their events: Joining legal organisations such as bar associations or legal societies, and attending their events and conferences can provide you with insights and information on the legal system and the latest trends, laws and procedures.

By taking these actionable steps, you can gain a deeper understanding of the legal system and procedures, and use this knowledge to make your crime novel more accurate and believable.

Remember to always fact-check your information and consider the legal jurisdiction of your story.

10

Violence In Crime Novels

Writing about violence in a crime novel can be a challenging task, as it requires balancing the need to create tension and suspense with the need to be mindful of the tone and level of violence in the story.

Here are a few actionable steps you can take to write about violence in a crime novel:

Be mindful of the tone: Consider the overall tone of your novel and how violence fits into it. If you are writing a hard-boiled noir story, violence may be a more prominent aspect of the story, while in a psychological thriller, the build-up of tension may be more important than graphic violence.

Use violence sparingly: Avoid overusing violence in your story. Instead, use it strategically to create tension and advance the plot. The use of violence should have a purpose, not just for the sake of it.

Consider the impact of violence on the characters: Think about how violence will affect the characters in your story, both physically and emotionally. Show the consequences of violence, both for the perpetrator and the victim.

Be mindful of the level of violence: Be mindful of the level of violence in your story and consider the potential impact it may have on your readers. While some readers may be comfortable with graphic violence, others may find it disturbing.

Use descriptive language carefully: Use descriptive language when writing about violence, but be mindful of how graphic it is. Don't go into too much detail, but enough to convey the violence without crossing any boundaries.

Research: If you are writing about a specific type of violence, such as gun violence or domestic abuse, it's important to research and understand the subject matter. This will help you to write about it authentically and responsibly.

The level of violence used in some common subgenres of crime fiction and why

Noir: Noir fiction is known for its gritty and violent tone. Noir novels often feature hard-boiled detectives and femme fatales, and the violence is often portrayed as a necessary evil in the pursuit of justice. Noir novels often include graphic descriptions of violence and may feature graphic scenes of murder and other crimes.

Cozy: The violence in cozy novels is often more subdued and less graphic, and the focus is more on the puzzle-solving aspect of the story rather than the violence itself.

Psychological: Psychological crime fiction often delves into the inner workings of the criminal mind and can be quite intense and disturbing. The violence in psychological novels can be graphic and may include detailed descriptions of violent acts.

Legal: The violence in legal novels is often less graphic and more focused on the legal proceedings and courtroom scenes.

Police procedural: The violence in police procedural novels can be graphic, but it is often more focused on the investigation than the violence itself.

Serial Killer: Serial killer novels focus on the actions and motivations of serial killers. The violence can be gory and these types of novels and/or movies tend to have trigger warnings.

11

Plotting or Pantsing?

When it comes to novel writing, there are two main approaches to developing a story: **plotting** and **pantsing.**

Plotting is the process of creating an outline or plan for the story before writing it. This approach involves taking the time to develop the plot, characters, and structure of the story before beginning to write.

Plotting can help writers to stay on track and avoid getting stuck in the middle of the story. This method is more suited for writers who like to have a clear structure and direction in their writing.

Pantsing, on the other hand, is the process of writing by the "seat of one's pants." This approach involves starting to write the story without a clear plan or outline. The writer starts with a general idea and then lets the story unfold as they write. This method is more suited for writers who like to be surprised by their own story and prefer to discover it as they go.

Both methods have their advantages and disadvantages. Plotting can help to ensure that the story stays on track and makes sense, while pantsing can lead to a more organic and spontaneous story development.

It's up to the writer to choose the method that works best for them. Some writers may even use a combination of both methods, starting with a basic outline and then letting the story develop as they write.

12

Point Of View In Novel Writing

Point of view (POV) in novel writing refers to the perspective from which a story is told. The point of view can be in first person, second person, or third person.

First person point of view: The narrator is a character in the story and uses "I" or "we" to describe the events. Example: *"I watched as the killer slipped away into the night."*

Second person point of view: The narrator addresses the reader directly as "you," making the reader a character in the story. Example: *"You follow the suspect through the crowded streets, never letting him out of your sight."*

Third person point of view: The narrator is not a character in the story and uses "he," "she," or "they" to describe the events. There are two types of third person point of view:

Third person limited: The narrator only has access to one character's thoughts and feelings. Example: *"She watched as the killer slipped away into the night, her heart racing with fear."*

Third person omniscient: The narrator has access to the thoughts and feelings of all characters in the story. Example: *"He watched as the killer slipped away into the night, his heart racing with fear. Meanwhile the detective was piecing together the clues to catch the killer"*

The choice of point of view can greatly affect the tone and style of a story, and can also affect the readers' level of engagement and empathy with the characters.

13

Coming Up With A Crime Idea For Your Novel

Coming up with a crime for your novel can be a challenging task, but there are a few things you can do to help generate ideas and develop a compelling story:

Research real-life crimes: This can be a great starting point for your novel. You can find inspiration in the details of real-life crimes, such as the methods used, the motives behind them, and the outcomes. This research can help you create a believable and realistic crime for your novel.

Consider the motivations and desires of your characters: Your crime should be closely tied to the characters in your novel. Think about what motivates them, what they want and what they are willing to do to get it. This can help you come up with a crime that is closely tied to the characters, and that the reader can understand and relate to.

Some ideas for motives

Greed and financial gain: The desire for money, inheritance, or property.

Revenge: Seeking revenge for a perceived wrong or injustice.

Jealousy: Envy over a relationship, love, or career success.

Mental illness: A person with a history of mental illness or instability may commit murder as a result of their condition.

Love and obsession: An individual may commit murder in order to be with or possess the person they are obsessed with.

Power and control: The desire to exert control and power over another person or situation.

Drug addiction or criminal activities: A person may commit murder to acquire drugs or money for their addiction or criminal activities.

Self-defence: A person may commit murder in what they perceive as self-defence or protection of themselves or loved ones.

Political or ideological motives: A person may commit murder for political or ideological reasons.

Cover-up: An individual may commit murder in order to conceal another crime, such as embezzlement or fraud.

It's important to note that motives for murder can be complex and multi-layered, and a criminal may have several motives that drive them to commit the crime.

Brainstorm different types of crime: Think about the

different types of crime you could use in your novel. For example, murder, theft, fraud, embezzlement, extortion, etc. Decide which type of crime would be most interesting and fitting for your story.

Create a list of suspects: Once you have decided on a crime, create a list of suspects. It can be helpful to have a few red herrings in the mix so that the reader is kept guessing until the end.

Some ideas to get you started:

- The victim's spouse or significant other who stands to gain financially from their death.
- The victim's business partner with a motive for getting rid of them.
- A jealous ex-lover who can't let go of the relationship.
- A family member with a history of mental illness or financial troubles.
- A neighbour with a grudge against the victim.
- A professional rival or colleague with a motive for taking the victim down.
- A hired hitman or professional criminal.
- A handyman or repair person who had access to the victim's home.
- A criminal organisation or gang with a connection to the victim.
- A seemingly innocent acquaintance with a secret motive or alibi.

These are just a few examples and it's important to keep in mind that the suspect can be anyone, it can be the most unexpected person.

Think about the location: The location of the crime can be just as important as the crime itself. Think about where the crime could take place and how it would affect the story.

Plan the investigation: Once you have the crime and suspects in place, think about how the investigation will unfold. Consider how the detective or investigator will gather clues and interview suspects, and what obstacles they may face along the way.

Add complexity and depth to the crime: Make sure your crime is not too simplistic or straightforward. Add complexity and depth to the crime by making the motive for the crime more complex, or by adding layers to the investigation.

Review and edit your crime: Once you have a rough draft of your crime, read it over and make sure it is believable and fits within the context of your novel. Make sure that all the elements of the crime (motive, suspects, investigation) are interconnected and contribute to the story.

14

Plotting And Structuring Your Novel

When plotting and structuring a crime story, it can be helpful to follow a general structure that includes the following elements:

The crime: The story should begin with the crime that sets the plot in motion. This could be a murder, theft, or any other criminal act that the investigation centres around.

The investigation: The investigation should be the main focus of the story and should include the actions and decisions of the main characters as they try to solve the crime.

The suspects: The suspects should be introduced early in the story and their actions and alibis should be examined as the investigation progresses.

The twist: A twist or revelation in the story can add an element of surprise and keep readers engaged.

The resolution: The story should end with the resolution of the crime and the capture of the perpetrator.

It is also important to consider the pacing of the story and to include both action and suspense to keep readers engaged. A variety of perspectives, such as the point of view of the detective and the perpetrator, can also add depth to the story.

It's also good to note that crime novel can have different structures such as inversion structure, multiple perspectives, and even non-linear. It all depends on the story you want to tell.

Your novel outline

Creating an outline for a novel can be a helpful way to organise your thoughts and plan out the structure of the story.

Here are some questions that can help you to create an effective outline for your novel:

- What is the overall premise or concept of the story?
- Who is the main character and what are their goals and motivations?
- Who are the other important characters and what roles do they play in the story?
- What is the inciting incident that sets the story in motion?
- What are the major conflicts and obstacles that the main character will face?
- What is the climax of the story and how does it resolve the main conflicts?
- What is the resolution of the story and how do the characters' arcs come to a close?
- How will the story be divided into acts or chapters?
- What are some key scenes or events that need to be included in the story?
- What is the theme or message of the story?
- What kind of tone or atmosphere do you want to create with the story?

- What are the research or background information you need to include in the story?
- Are there any elements of subplots that you want to include in the story?
- What are the main sources of tension and conflict in the story?

Example of a basic novel outline you can use

The three-act structure, as previously mentioned, is a common method for outlining a novel, and it can help to ensure that your story has a clear and satisfying structure.

Here are some actionable steps you can take to create a novel outline using the three-act structure:

Act 1: The Setup. This is where you introduce the main character, the setting, and the main conflict or problem that the character will face. You should also establish the character's goals and motivations, and introduce any important secondary characters.

Act 2: The Confrontation. This is where the main character confronts the main conflict or problem, and faces a series of obstacles and challenges. This act should also include a midpoint, which marks a turning point in the story and changes the character's goals or motivations.

Act 3: The Resolution. This is where the main character achieves their goals or resolves the main conflict. This act should also include a climax, which is the most intense and dramatic moment of the story, and a resolution, which brings the story to a close and ties up loose ends.

Divide the acts into chapters: Break down your three acts into chapters, and make sure that each chapter has a clear and specific purpose.

Determine the key scenes and events: For each act and chapter, identify the key scenes and events that need to be included in the story, and make sure that they are cohesive and serve the overall structure of the story.

Revise and edit: Once you have an outline, you can use it as a guide to write your novel and then revise and edit it as you go.

15

Creating A Compelling Opening Scene

Creating a compelling opening scene for a crime novel is crucial in setting the tone for the story and making the readers want to keep reading.

Here are some actionable steps you can take to create a compelling opening scene for a crime novel:

Start with a strong hook: A strong hook can be a glimpse of the crime, a question about the crime, a short dialogue that hints at the crime, or a mysterious image that implies a crime.

Introduce interesting characters: Introduce your main characters, including the detective and the suspect, in the opening scene. Show their personalities, their quirks, and their goals. Make the readers care about them and want to know more.

Create a sense of tension or conflict: A sense of tension or conflict can make the opening scene more engaging. You can create tension by showing the crime scene or the aftermath of the crime. You can create conflict by introducing a character who is struggling with the crime or by setting up a confrontation between the detective and the suspect.

Use foreshadowing: Use foreshadowing to hint at the events that will occur later in the story. This can create a sense of anticipation and make the reader want to keep reading to find out what happens next.

Show the stakes: Make it clear what's at stake for the characters. It could be a murder, a missing person, a robbery, or something else, show the reader why it's important to the characters and why it's important to solve the crime.

Use descriptive language: Use descriptive language to create a sense of place and atmosphere, and consider the time period and location of your story.

16

Creating Characters

Creating believable and compelling characters is an important aspect of writing a successful novel.

Developing a detailed backstory and personality for your characters, as well as considering their goals and motivations, can help make them believable and compelling.

Here are some actionable tips and steps to help you create characters that readers will care about and remember:

Develop a detailed backstory: Every character has a history that shapes who they are and how they react to the events of the story. Take the time to create a detailed backstory for each of your characters, including their childhood, family, education, and past experiences. This will help you understand your characters better and make them feel more real to the reader.

Create a unique personality: Each character should have a unique personality that sets them apart from the others. Think about their likes, dislikes, strengths, weaknesses, and quirks. This will help you create a character who feels like a real person and not a stereotype.

Consider their goals and motivations: Every character should have a clear goal or motivation that drives them throughout the story. This goal or motivation should be something that the reader can understand and relate to. It can be related to their backstory and personality.

Give them contradictions: Characters should have contradictions, it makes them more interesting and realistic. For example, a character who is brave in the face of danger may be afraid of heights, or a character who is kind-hearted may have a short temper.

Create an arc for your characters: Characters should change and evolve throughout the story, it is called a character arc. It is the process of a character's growth and development throughout the story. The character's arc should be connected to the story's arc and the main theme of the novel.

Show, don't tell: When you are introducing your characters to the reader, it is better to show them in action and through their thoughts, words, and actions rather than telling the reader about their characteristics.

Use dialogue to reveal character: Dialogue is a powerful tool for revealing character. The way a character speaks can reveal a lot about their personality, background, and motivations.

Make them relatable: Characters should be relatable to the reader, meaning that the reader can understand and relate to their thoughts, feelings, and actions. This will help the reader to connect with the characters and care about what happens to them.

Be consistent: Once you have established your characters' personalities, goals, and motivations, be consistent in their behaviour throughout the story. Inconsistency can cause confusion and disconnection with the reader.

Review and Edit: Once you have a rough draft of your characters, read it over and make sure they are believable and consistent throughout the novel. Make sure they are connected to the story and the main theme of the novel.

Example: In J.K. Rowling's Harry Potter series, the character of Harry Potter has a detailed backstory, a unique personality, a clear goal and motivation which is to defeat Voldemort and a clear character arc as he matures and evolves throughout the series.

He has contradictions, for example, he is brave but also impulsive. He is relatable as the reader can understand and relate to his thoughts, feelings, and actions. His dialogue is used to reveal his character and his behaviour is consistent throughout the series.

Creating a believable detective character

Creating a believable detective character is an important aspect of writing a crime novel. A well-developed detective character can make the story more engaging and believable.

Here are some actionable steps you can take to create a believable detective character:

Consider the detective's backstory: A detective's backstory includes their upbringing, family, education, and past experiences that have shaped who they are. It's important to consider how their past experiences have influenced their personality and how it affects their work.

Develop the detective's personality: A detective's personality is an important aspect of their character. Consider the detective's traits, such as their sense of humour, their level of empathy, and their ability to connect with others. Think about how these traits affect their relationships with other characters and how they approach their work.

Decide on the detective's skills: A detective's skills are another important aspect of their character. Decide on their level of expertise in areas such as criminal investigations, forensic science, and interviewing. Consider how these skills help them solve cases and how they might impact their relationships with other characters.

Give the detective flaws and vulnerabilities: No one is perfect, and that includes detectives. Give your detective character flaws and vulnerabilities that make them human. It makes them relatable and believable.

Show the detective's growth: As the story progresses, show how the detective character develops and changes. Show how they learn from their mistakes, how they adapt to new situations, and how they grow as a person and as a detective.

Creating a believable suspect character

Creating a believable suspect character is an important aspect of writing a crime novel. A well-developed suspect character can add depth to the story and make the plot more engaging and believable.

Here are some actionable steps you can take to create a believable suspect character:

Consider the suspect's backstory: A suspect's backstory includes their upbringing, family, education, and past experiences that have shaped who they are. It's important to consider how their past experiences have influenced their personality and how it affects their actions.

Develop the suspect's personality: A suspect's personality is an important aspect of their character. Consider the suspect's traits, such as their level of empathy, their intelligence, and their ability to connect with others. Think about how these traits affect their relationships with other characters and how they approach their actions.

Decide on the suspect's motivations: A suspect's motivations are key in making them believable. Decide on the reasons why they committed the crime, whether it be greed, revenge, or a twisted sense of justice. Make sure their motivations are consistent with their personality and backstory.

Give the suspect flaws and vulnerabilities: Give your suspect character flaws and vulnerabilities that make them human. It makes them relatable and believable.

Show the suspect's growth: As the story progresses, show how the suspect character develops and changes. Show how they learn from their mistakes, how they adapt to new situations, and how they grow as a person and as a suspect.

Creating a full character profile

Creating a full character profile for a novel can be an important step in developing well-rounded and believable characters. Here are some character profile questions that can help you to create a full character profile:

- What is the character's name?
- What is the character's age?
- What is the character's occupation?
- What is the character's physical appearance?
- What is the character's personality?
- What are the character's goals and motivations?
- What is the character's backstory?
- What is the character's family and relationship history?

- What is the character's education and background?
- What are the character's strengths and weaknesses?
- What are the character's likes and dislikes?
- What are the character's values and beliefs?
- What is the character's role in the story?
- What is the character's arc in the story?
- What are some of the character's defining moments in the story?

By answering these questions, you can create a comprehensive and detailed character profile that will help you to understand your character and make them believable to your readers.

17

How To Incorporate Suspense In Your Crime Novel

Incorporating suspense in a crime novel is an essential part of the genre. Suspense is the feeling of uncertainty and anticipation that keeps the reader on the edge of their seat.

Here are some actionable steps you can take to incorporate suspense in your crime novel:

Use foreshadowing: Foreshadowing is a technique that hints at events that will occur later in the story. This can create a sense of anticipation and make the reader want to keep reading to find out what happens next. You can use foreshadowing in the form of hints, clues, or symbols that are revealed early on in the story, and then pay off later.

Use misdirection: Misdirection is a technique that leads the reader to believe something that is not true. This can create a sense of uncertainty and make the reader question what is real and what is not. This technique can be used to mislead the reader and keep them guessing about the true nature of the crime and the identity of the perpetrator.

Use pacing: Pacing refers to the speed at which the story unfolds. Varying the pacing can help to build suspense and keep the reader engaged. You can use a slower pace to build tension and a faster pace to increase the sense of urgency and danger.

Use cliffhangers: A cliffhanger is a dramatic device that leaves the reader in suspense at the end of a chapter or scene. This can create a sense of anticipation and make the reader want to keep reading to find out what happens next.

By using these techniques, you can create a sense of uncertainty and anticipation that will keep the reader engaged and wanting more.

Remember to keep the balance between suspense and revelation, too much suspense and no revelation can leave the reader frustrated, and too much revelation with no suspense can make the story predictable.

18

How To Create A Sense Of Place And Atmosphere In Your Writing

Creating a sense of place and atmosphere in writing is an important aspect of storytelling. It helps the reader to visualise the setting, and understand the mood and tone of the story.

Here are some actionable steps you can take to create a sense of place and atmosphere in your writing:

Use descriptive language: To create a sense of place, use descriptive language to describe the setting. Use specific details such as the architecture, the colours, the textures, the sounds, the smells, and the weather. This will help the reader to visualise the setting and feel like they are there.

Consider the time period and location of your story: Knowing the historical context and cultural background of the time period and location where your story takes place will help you to create a more authentic and believable setting. Researching the customs, the traditions, and the social norms of the time and place will give you a deeper understanding of the setting and help you to create a more accurate and convincing atmosphere.

Show the characters' perspectives: Characters have their own perspectives on the setting. By showing their perspectives and how they interact with the setting, it creates a sense of immersion for the reader.

Use sensory details: Think about how the setting makes the characters feel. Use sensory details to convey the emotions the setting evokes in the characters. For example, if the setting is a dark and gloomy forest, you might use words like "dreary" and "foreboding" to create a sense of unease and fear.

Use figurative language: Figurative language can be used to create atmosphere and mood. For example, you might use metaphors or similes to describe the setting in a way that evokes a particular emotion or atmosphere.

By following these actionable steps, you can create a sense of place and atmosphere in your writing that will help to engage the reader and make the story more vivid and believable.

19

Plot Twists

Q: What is a plot twist and why is it important in a novel?

A: A plot twist is a sudden and unexpected turn of events in a story that changes the direction or outcome of the plot. It is an element of fiction writing that aims to keep the readers engaged, by catching them off guard and making them question what they thought they knew about the story.

Plot twists are important in a novel because they create tension, suspense, and surprise, which can make the story more engaging and memorable for the reader.

Q: How can an author effectively create a plot twist in a novel?

A: An author can effectively create a plot twist in a novel by using the following techniques:

Planting seeds of doubt: An author can plant small hints or clues throughout the story that may suggest something is not as it seems. This can make the plot twist more satisfying when it is finally revealed.

Using foreshadowing: An author can use foreshadowing to hint at the plot twist, but not reveal it directly. This can create a sense of unease and anticipation in the reader, making the plot twist more effective.

Creating a believable and logical twist: A plot twist should be believable and logical, even if it is unexpected. It should come from the story's internal logic and not just appear out of the blue.

Making the twist surprising but not too convoluted: A plot twist should be surprising, but it should not be so convoluted that it becomes unbelievable or hard to follow.

Addressing the twist and its consequences: After the twist is revealed, an author should address its consequences and how it changes the story.
Example: In the novel "The Girl on the Train" by Paula Hawkins, the plot twist is revealed when the main character discovers that her ex-husband, who she thought was cheating on her, was actually innocent and she had been falsely accusing him. This plot twist is effective because it is surprising and logical, and it changes the direction of the story and the reader's understanding of the characters.

Q: How can an author use plot twists to create a satisfying ending for a novel?

A: An author can use plot twists to create a satisfying ending for a novel by using the following techniques:

Resolving conflicts: A plot twist can be used to resolve conflicts in the story, and bring a sense of closure to the reader.

Giving characters a sense of growth and change: A plot

twist can be used to give characters a sense of growth and change, and make their journey feel meaningful.

Reflecting the themes of the story: A plot twist can be used to reflect the themes of the story, and make the ending feel satisfying and thought-provoking.

Example: In the novel "The Sixth Sense" by M. Night Shyamalan, the plot twist is revealed at the end of the story when the main character discovers that he is dead. This plot twist is effective because it resolves the conflict of the story, gives the character a sense of growth and change, and reflects the themes of the story.

Overall, plot twists can be a powerful tool for adding depth and intrigue to a novel. When used effectively, they can create tension, suspense, and surprise for the reader, and lead to a satisfying and memorable ending.

20

Red Herrings

In a crime novel, a red herring is a plot device used to mislead the reader or the characters in the story. It is a false clue or information that leads the characters and readers away from the true culprit or solution of the crime.

The use of red herrings is common in detective novels and can add an element of surprise and uncertainty to the plot. It is often used to keep the reader guessing until the climax of the story when the true perpetrator is revealed.

Incorporating red herrings, or false clues or suspects, in a crime novel can be an effective way to build suspense. Here are some actionable steps you can take to incorporate red herrings in your crime novel:

Decide on the red herrings: Decide on the red herrings you want to include in your story. They can be physical clues, such as a weapon or an alibi, or they can be characters, such as a suspect who appears guilty but is later cleared.

Plant the red herrings early: Plant the red herrings early in the story, so that the reader is led to believe that they are important to the case. This will create a sense of anticipation and make the reader want to keep reading to find out more.

Make the red herrings believable: The red herrings should be believable and consistent with the story and the characters. They should not be too obvious or too far-fetched.

Use misdirection: Use misdirection to mislead the reader or the detective. This can be done by emphasising certain clues or suspects, while downplaying others.

Reveal the red herrings at the right time: Reveal the red herrings at the right time in the story. Don't reveal them too early, or the reader will lose interest. But don't reveal them too late, or the reader will feel cheated.

Keep the red herrings relevant to the story: Keep the red herrings relevant to the story and the characters, even if they are not directly related to the crime. This will add depth and complexity to the story.

21

Using Descriptive Language

Writing descriptive language in a crime novel can be a powerful tool for revealing information about the characters and the story.

Here are a few actionable steps you can take to write effective descriptive language in a crime novel:

Create a sense of place: Use descriptive language to create a vivid and detailed picture of the setting in which the story takes place. This can include physical descriptions of buildings, streets, and landscapes, as well as details about the weather and the time of day.

Use descriptive language to create atmosphere: Use descriptive language to create a mood or feeling associated with the setting. For example, you can use descriptive language to create a sense of dread or unease in a dark and gloomy alleyway, or a sense of warmth and comfort in a cozy living room.

Use descriptive language to reveal information about the characters: Use descriptive language to reveal information about the physical appearance, mannerisms, and personalities of the characters. This can help readers to understand and connect with the characters.

Use descriptive language to reveal information about the story: Use descriptive language to reveal information about the crime, clues, and suspects. It can help to set the tone and pacing of the story.

Use sensory details: Use descriptive language to convey the sights, sounds, smells, tastes, and textures of the setting and the characters. This can help to create a more immersive and believable world for the reader.

Be selective with descriptive language: Be mindful of the amount of descriptive language used. It's important not to overdo it as it can slow down the pacing and take away from the plot. Use descriptive language strategically, to highlight the most important aspects of the story and characters.

22

Writing Dialogue In A Crime Novel

Writing dialogue in a crime novel can be a powerful tool for revealing character traits, advancing the plot, and keeping the reader engaged.

Here are a few actionable steps you can take to write effective dialogue in a crime novel:

Make the dialogue sound natural: The dialogue should be written in a way that sounds like real people speaking. Avoid using overly formal or stilted language, and instead focus on creating conversations that feel authentic.

Reveal character traits through dialogue: Use dialogue to reveal the personalities, motivations, and backgrounds of the characters. For example, a character who speaks in a formal and precise manner might be a lawyer, while a character who uses slang and curse words might be a street-wise detective.

Use dialogue to advance the plot: Dialogue should be used to reveal important information about the story, such as clues to the crime or the suspects' alibis. Characters should also use dialogue to discuss their suspicions, theories and plans.

Use subtext: Subtext is the unspoken thoughts and emotions behind a character's words. Use subtext to create tension and suspense, and make the dialogue more interesting.

Using different types of dialogue

Interrogation: This is when characters are questioning suspects or witnesses. Use this type of dialogue to reveal information and clues about the crime.

Confrontation: This is when characters are arguing or having a heated confrontation. Use this type of dialogue to reveal tensions and conflicts between characters.

Small talk: This is when characters are having casual conversations. Use this type of dialogue to reveal character backgrounds and relationships

Using dialogue to advance the plot

Effective use of dialogue in a novel can be a powerful tool for conveying character development and advancing the plot. Here are a few ways an author can use dialogue to achieve these goals:

Use dialogue to reveal a character's personality: A character's words and the way they speak can reveal a lot about their personality, emotions, and motivations. For example, a character who speaks in a formal, polite manner may be hiding something, while a character who speaks in a harsh, confrontational manner may be struggling with anger or insecurity.

Use dialogue to reveal a character's backstory: A character's words and the way they speak can also reveal their backstory and history. For example, a character who speaks with a strong accent or uses specific colloquialisms may be from a specific region or have a unique cultural background.

Use dialogue to advance the plot: Dialogue can be used to move the plot forward by revealing new information, introducing conflict, or propelling the story in a new direction. For example, a conversation between two characters may reveal a secret that changes the course of the story, or a confrontation between two characters may lead to a turning point in the plot.

Use subtext in dialogue: Subtext is the underlying meaning or implication behind a character's words. It can be used to reveal a character's true thoughts or feelings, or to create tension or conflict between characters.

Use silence and non-verbal communication: In addition to spoken dialogue, silence and non-verbal communication can be just as powerful in conveying character development and advancing the plot. For example, a character who refuses to speak or avoids eye contact may be hiding something or feeling ashamed, while a character who speaks softly or hesitantly may be uncertain or insecure.

Overall, the key to effectively using dialogue in a novel is to use it in a way that is true to the characters and their personalities, and to use it to reveal information, introduce conflict, and advance the plot.

How to use dialogue in a novel with regards to gender

Using dialogue to convey gender in a novel can be a powerful tool for creating realistic and nuanced characters. Here are a few ways an author can use dialogue to convey gender in a novel:

Use gendered language and speech patterns: Men and women often use different language and speech patterns, such as different forms of address and different types of vocabulary. By using these gendered language patterns in dialogue, an author can create a sense of authenticity for their male and female characters.

Use interruptions and talk-overs: Research shows that in many cultures, men are more likely to interrupt and talk over women in conversations. An author can use this phenomenon in their dialogue to convey power dynamics between male and female characters.

Use different dialogue styles to reflect gendered expectations: Society often has different expectations of how men and women should speak and interact. An author can use these expectations in their dialogue to convey character development. For example, a female character who speaks assertively and confidently may challenge societal expectations and be seen as a strong and independent woman.

Use gendered idioms: Some idioms and expressions are gendered in their origin and use, for example "man up" "like a girl" etc. Using them can reflect the gender biases and stereotypes of the character, whether they align with them or challenge them.

Be mindful of intersectionality: Gender is not the only factor that shapes how people communicate, other factors such as race, ethnicity, sexual orientation, and socioeconomic status also play a role. An author should be mindful of these factors and how they may shape their characters' dialogue.

It's important to note that these are generalisations and not all men or women conform to them, however, using them can help in creating an authentic and relatable characters. An author should also be aware of their own biases when writing dialogue, and strive to create characters that are complex and multifaceted.

Dialogue in a novel with regards to pacing

Using dialogue in a novel to convey pacing is a powerful tool for creating a sense of tension and excitement in a story. Here are a few ways an author can use dialogue to control pacing in a novel, specifically in a panic scene:

Use short, staccato sentences: In a panic scene, characters may be speaking quickly and urgently. Using short, staccato sentences in the dialogue can convey a sense of haste and urgency, and increase the pace of the scene.

Use incomplete sentences and fragments: Characters in a panic scene may be so focused on the immediate situation that they don't have time to complete their thoughts. Using incomplete sentences and fragments in the dialogue can convey a sense of disorientation and confusion, which can help to increase the pace of the scene.

Use repetition: Characters in a panic scene may be repeating themselves or asking the same questions over and over. Using repetition in the dialogue can convey a sense of fear and confusion, and increase the pace of the scene.

Use exclamations and interjections: Characters in a panic scene may be yelling or exclaiming in fear or shock. Using exclamations and interjections in the dialogue can convey a sense of panic and urgency, and increase the pace of the scene.

Use silence: In a panic scene, characters may be so focused on their immediate surroundings that they don't have time to speak. Using silence in the dialogue can convey a sense of tension and unease, and increase the pace of the scene.

Use short paragraphs: Breaking the dialogue into short paragraphs can help to increase the pace of the scene, as it creates a sense of immediacy and urgency.

Use active verbs: Using active verbs in dialogue can help to convey a sense of movement and action, which can help to increase the pace of the scene.

It's important to note that in a panic scene, less words are used, as characters might not have the time or the ability to express themselves fully. Using the above techniques can help an author to control the pacing in a panic scene, and create a sense of tension and excitement for the reader

Show not tell

"Show not tell" is a writing technique that encourages writers to use descriptive and sensory language to "show" the reader what is happening, rather than simply "telling" them. This technique is used in all forms of writing, but it is particularly important in fiction writing as it allows the reader to experience the story in a more immersive and engaging way.

When writing, it is easy to fall into the trap of telling the reader what is happening, rather than showing them. Telling can take the form of using words like *"he felt," "she thought,"* or *"they saw."* These words often indicate that the writer is summarising the action or providing information to the reader, rather than allowing them to experience the scene.

An example of "telling" would be: *"She was feeling angry and sad."*

An example of "showing" would be: *"She clenched her fists and felt the hot tears streaming down her face."*

The "show" version not only tells us the emotion of the character but also gives us an action that indicates that emotion, making it more vivid and real.

Another example of "telling" would be: *"He was a kind man."*

An example of "showing" would be: *"He always put others before himself, even when it meant going without."*

By using "show" the author is giving us an action that indicates the kindness of the character.

When using "show not tell", the writer should focus on using descriptive language to create vivid and detailed images in the reader's mind. This can include using sensory details, such as sight, sound, taste, touch, and smell, to create a more immersive and realistic experience for the reader. It's also important to use action and dialogue to reveal characters' emotions and thoughts, rather than simply telling the reader what they are feeling or thinking.

For example, instead of saying *"he was feeling nervous,"* the writer could show the character fidgeting with his hands or sweating profusely, indicating that he is nervous. Instead of saying *"she was feeling happy,"* the writer could show the character smiling or laughing, indicating that she is happy.

Another example of "showing" would be: *"She walked into the room and looked around, taking in the fancy chandeliers and the white-clothed tables. The sound of clinking glasses and chatter filled her ears as she made her way to the bar."* This passage uses descriptive language and sensory details to create a vivid and detailed image of the scene for the reader, allowing them to experience it for themselves.

23

How To End Your Novel

Creating a believable resolution for your crime novel is essential for making the story satisfying and believable for the reader.

A good ending for a novel is one that feels fitting for the story, characters and themes. Good endings should include the following elements:

Tie up loose ends: The ending should tie up all the loose ends in the story, including the details of the crime, the clues and evidence, and the characters' arcs. Make sure that all the conflicts presented in the story is resolved and that the reader has a clear understanding of what happened.

Provide a resolution to the crime: The ending should provide a resolution to the crime and the perpetrator should be caught or brought to justice. The reader should have a clear understanding of the crime and how it was solved.

Make sure the resolution is logical: The resolution should be based on the information that has been presented in the story, and it should make sense. The clues and evidence should be consistent with the resolution, and it should be clear how they led to the perpetrator being caught.

Provide a resolution to the characters' arcs: The ending should provide a resolution to the characters' arcs, including the detective, the suspects, and the victim. Show how the characters have grown, changed, and been impacted by the crime.

Consider all the characters: The resolution should take into account all the characters in the story, including the victim, the detective, and the suspects. The resolution should be fair to all the characters and not come out of left field.

Keep it satisfying: The resolution should be satisfying for the reader. It should provide closure for the story, and it should be emotionally satisfying, whether it's a happy or tragic ending.

Use foreshadowing: Consider using foreshadowing to set up the resolution. This can help to make the resolution more believable, as the reader will have been prepared for it.

Avoid clichés: Try to avoid using clichéd resolutions, such as the "twist ending" or the "surprise suspect." These types of endings can be predictable and unsatisfying for the reader.

Show the aftermath: Show the aftermath of the crime, and how it affects the characters and the community. This will give the story a sense of closure and realism.

Use descriptive language: Use descriptive language to create a sense of place and atmosphere, and consider the time period and location of your story.

Reflecting themes: A good ending should reflect the themes of the story, making the ending feel meaningful and thought-provoking.

Being true to the story: An author should stay true to the story, and not force an ending that feels unnatural or contrived.

Giving characters a sense of growth and change: A good ending should give characters a sense of growth and change, making their journey feel meaningful.

Being memorable: A good ending should be memorable, leaving a lasting impression on the reader.

Example: In the novel "To Kill a Mockingbird" by Harper Lee, the ending brings a sense of closure to the story's main conflict of racism and prejudice. The themes of the book are reflected in the final lines of the story, and the main character, Scout, has grown and changed throughout the story. The ending is memorable, and stays with the reader long after the book is finished.

Creating a satisfying and fitting ending for a novel

An author can create a satisfying and fitting ending for a novel by using the following techniques:

Planning the ending: An author should have a clear idea of how the story will end before they begin writing.

Building towards the ending: An author should use foreshadowing and other techniques to build towards the ending, making it feel like a natural progression of the story.

Example: In the novel "The Great Gatsby" by F. Scott Fitzgerald, the ending is fitting and satisfying because it reflects the themes of the story, such as the corruption of the American Dream and the consequences of excess. The characters have also undergone significant growth and change throughout the story, and the ending feels like a natural progression of the story.

Using different types of endings

An author can use different types of endings to create a memorable and impactful ending for a novel, such as:

Open endings: An open ending leaves the story unresolved and open to interpretation, allowing readers to form their own conclusions.

Cliffhanger endings: A cliffhanger ending leaves the story unresolved, leaving readers eager for a sequel or the next instalment.

Surprise endings: A surprise ending is an unexpected and shocking ending that catches readers off guard.

Tragic endings: A tragic ending involves the death or downfall of the main character, leaving a lasting emotional impact on the reader.

Happy endings: A happy ending provides a sense of closure and satisfaction for the reader.

Example: In the novel "The Hunger Games" by Suzanne Collins, the ending is impactful because it is a mix of a surprise and a tragic ending. The main character, Katniss, survives the Hunger Games, but some of her loved ones and friends don't.

24

Crime Novel Book Titles

Here are some tips on how to come up with an enticing book title:

Use descriptive words: Use words that evoke emotion and give a sense of what the story is about, for example "Deadly Secrets," "Killer Instinct," or "Murderous Minds."

Play with puns: Use puns or wordplay to create a clever and memorable title, such as "Murder She Wrote," "Death Knell," or "Killing Time."

Use quotes or phrases: Use a quote or phrase from the story, or one that relates to the theme or plot, such as "Whodunit," "The Silence of the Lambs," or "The Girl with the Dragon Tattoo."

Use the names of characters: Use the name of the main character, antagonist, or location as the title, such as "The Jack Reacher series," "The Lincoln Rhyme series," or "The Girl on the Train."

Use symbolism: Use symbolism or imagery that relates to the story, such as "The Haunting of Hill House," "The Black Dahlia," or "The Name of the Rose."

Be mysterious: Create a sense of intrigue and mystery with your title, such as "The Vanishing," "The Unseen," or "The Unknown."

Keep it simple: Sometimes simple and straightforward titles can be the most effective, such as "The Murder of Roger Ackroyd" by Agatha Christie, "The Silence of the Lambs" by Thomas Harris.

Get creative: Feel free to experiment with different styles of titles and don't be afraid to think outside the box, such as "The Red Herring" by D. L. Sayers

25

Crime Writing Word Count

The word count for a crime novel can vary greatly, and there is no set standard for what is considered an appropriate word count. A crime novel can be anywhere from 50,000 words to 100,000 words or more.

Typically, a crime novel will fall within the range of 80,000 to 100,000 words, but it really depends on the story, the writing style, and the intended audience. Some crime novels may be shorter and more focused on a single crime or investigation, while others may be longer and more complex, spanning multiple investigations and characters over a longer period of time.

It is important to note that the word count is not the most important aspect of a novel, what is important is that the story is well-told, engaging and satisfying for the reader. If a author is able to tell a compelling story in a shorter word count, it can be just as effective as a longer one. And vice versa, if the author is not able to keep the readers interest, a longer word count won't save the novel.

It's important for the author to focus on telling the best story possible and finding the appropriate word count that allows them to do that.

26

Crime Fiction Book Cover Tips

Let's dive straight in to the most common questions asked when it comes to book covers:

Q: What is the purpose of a book cover?

A: The purpose of a book cover is to grab the reader's attention and entice them to pick up the book. A good book cover should also give an idea of what the book is about and what genre it belongs to. A well-designed cover can also contribute to the book's overall aesthetic and branding.

Q: What elements should be included in a book cover design?

A: A good book cover design should include the following elements:

Title and author name: These are the most important elements of a book cover, as they identify the book and its author.

Image or illustration: A good book cover should have an image or illustration that is relevant to the book's story or theme.

Typography: The text should be legible and easy to read, with a font that is appropriate for the book's genre and style.

Colour scheme: The colour scheme should be consistent with the book's genre and style, and should complement the image or illustration.

Branding: If the book is part of a series, the cover should be consistent with the branding of the previous books in the series.

Q: Why are good book covers important?

A: Good book covers are important because they:

Entice readers: A good book cover can grab the reader's attention and entice them to pick up the book and read it.

Represent the book's content: A good book cover should give an idea of what the book is about and what genre it belongs to.

Contribute to the book's overall aesthetic: A well-designed cover can contribute to the book's overall aesthetic and branding.

Increase book sales: A good book cover can increase book sales, as it can make the book more attractive and desirable to readers.

Help the book stand out: A good book cover can help the book stand out from others on a bookstore shelf or online.

Example: The cover of "The Girl on the Train" by Paula Hawkins features an illustration of a train in motion, with the title and author name in a bold and easy-to-read font. The cover is consistent with the book's genre (psychological thriller), and the image of the train is relevant to the book's story. The colours and design of the cover also contribute to the book's overall aesthetic and branding.

Considerations when planning your crime novel book cover

- Use a striking image that immediately evokes the crime genre, such as a silhouette of a criminal, a weapon, or a crime scene.
- Incorporate symbolic elements that hint at the themes or plot of the book, such as a cityscape for a crime novel set in a urban area, or a fingerprint for a story about forensic science.
- Use a bold, contrasting colour scheme to make the cover stand out on a bookshelf or online store.
- Incorporate typography that is clear, easy to read, and fits with the overall aesthetic of the cover.
- Consider using a tagline or a clever play on words to entice readers.
- Think about the target audience and try to design a cover that appeals to them.
- Use high-quality images, with good resolution and lighting, to create a professional look.
- Use negative space effectively to create a sense of mystery or suspense.
- Try to avoid overcrowding the cover with too many elements or text.
- Use a consistent style throughout the series if the book is part of a series.

27

Editors

Q: What are the different types of editors and what do they do?

A: There are several types of editors, each with a specific focus and set of responsibilities. These include:

Developmental editor: A developmental editor works with the author to shape the overall structure, plot, characters, and themes of the novel. They help the author to make the story coherent and compelling.

Line editor: A line editor works with the author to refine the language and make sure it is clear, concise and engaging. They focus on grammar, punctuation, and wording.

Copyeditor: A copyeditor focuses on the manuscript's mechanics, such as spelling, punctuation, grammar, and consistency. They help the author to ensure that the manuscript is free of errors and ready for publication.

Proofreader: A proofreader is the final stage of editing, and is done after the manuscript has been typeset. They look for any remaining errors in spelling, punctuation, grammar, and formatting.

Content editor: A content editor focuses on the overall content of the manuscript, ensuring that it flows well, is consistent and error-free. They work with the author to identify any issues with pacing, continuity, and characters development.

Sensitivity editor: A sensitivity editor focuses on ensuring that the content of the manuscript is culturally sensitive and respectful, and does not offend any particular group of people.

28

Book Marketing

Here are the most common questions asked about book marketing:

Q: Where should beginner authors go to market their book?

A: Beginner authors can market their book through a variety of channels, including:

Social media: Social media platforms such as Facebook, Twitter, Instagram, and Goodreads can be used to connect with readers, build a following, and promote the book.

Online bookstores: Online bookstores such as Amazon and Barnes & Noble can be used to sell the book and reach a wide audience.

Blogs and websites: Blogs and websites such as Medium, Tumblr, and WordPress can be used to share information about the book, post reviews, and connect with readers.

Book clubs and reading groups: Joining book clubs and

reading groups can be a great way for beginner authors to connect with readers and promote their book.

Bookstores and libraries: Pitching to bookstores and libraries can be a great way to get your book in front of readers.

Book festivals and events: Attending book festivals and events can be a great way to connect with readers and other authors.

Q: What should beginner authors spend on book marketing?

A: The amount a beginner author should spend on book marketing will vary depending on their budget and the marketing channels they choose to use.

Some marketing channels, such as social media, are relatively low-cost, while others, such as advertising, can be more expensive.

It's important for beginner authors to be mindful of their budget and to prioritise the marketing channels that will be most effective for their book and target audience.

Some authors may choose to invest more in online advertising or social media marketing, while others may prefer to focus on building relationships with bookstores and libraries, or attending book festivals and events.

It's also important to note that there are some free or low-cost options for book marketing, such as utilising free tools on social media, reaching out to book reviewers, or participating in online book clubs and reading groups.

29

Crime Writing Glossary

Alibi: An excuse or proof that a suspect was somewhere else at the time a crime was committed.
Example: *"The suspect had a solid alibi for the night of the murder, having been at a business conference in another city."*

Caper: A type of crime fiction that focuses on a group of criminals planning and executing a heist or other daring crime.
Example: *"The caper novel followed a team of expert thieves as they pulled off the perfect heist."*

Clues: Evidence or information that helps to solve a crime.
Example: *"The detective followed a trail of clues that led him to the real killer."*

Cold case: A crime that remains unsolved for a long period of time, often being reopened and investigated again by police.
Example: *"The detective was tasked with solving a cold case murder that had stumped investigators for years."*

Cozy: A type of crime fiction that is characterised by its focus on

small towns, amateur sleuths, and a lack of graphic violence or explicit sex.
Example: *"The cozy mystery was set in a picturesque village where the local bookstore owner helped to solve the case."*

Crime scene: The location where a crime took place, including any physical evidence or clues related to the crime.
Example: *"The detective carefully examined the crime scene for any clues that could lead to the perpetrator."*

Cross examination: The process of questioning a witness in a trial to challenge their testimony or credibility.
Example: *"The defence attorney's cross examination revealed that the witness's testimony was unreliable."*

Dead end: A lead or piece of evidence that does not lead to any further progress in an investigation.
Example: *"The detective hit a dead end in the case, but refused to give up until the killer was caught."*

Deep cover: An undercover operation in which the undercover agent becomes fully immersed in the criminal organisation they are investigating.
Example: *"The detective went deep cover to infiltrate the dangerous gang and gather evidence against them."*

Detective fiction: A type of crime fiction that focuses on the process of solving a crime, often featuring detectives or police officers as the main characters.
Example: *"The detective fiction novel followed the brilliant detective as he worked to solve a string of murders."*

False confession: A confession to a crime that the person did not actually commit.
Example: *"The suspect's false confession led the detective down the wrong path, delaying the true resolution of the case."*

Forensics: The scientific examination and analysis of physical evidence in relation to a crime.
Example: *"Forensic evidence found at the crime scene pointed to the defendant as the killer."*

Frame-up: A situation in which someone is deliberately set up to take the blame for a crime they did not commit.
Example: *"The detective uncovered a frame-up, realising that the real killer had set up an innocent person to take the fall."*

Gun moll: A female criminal associated with a male gangster, often as his romantic partner.
Example: *"The gun moll was the mastermind behind the heist, using her charm and beauty to distract the guards while her accomplices made off with the loot."*

Hard-Boiled: A type of crime fiction characterised by its tough, no-nonsense protagonist and fast-paced, action-packed storylines.
Example: *"The hard-boiled detective dug deep into the criminal underworld to bring the killer to justice."*

Hunch: An instinct or feeling that something is true, often based on limited or circumstantial evidence.
Example: *"The detective had a hunch that the suspect was hiding something, and was determined to get to the bottom of it."*

Immunity deal: A legal agreement in which a suspect agrees to testify in exchange for immunity from prosecution for their own crimes.
Example: *"The immunity deal allowed the detective to get the testimony he needed to finally solve the case."*

Inside man: A criminal who has infiltrated a legal organisation, often for the purpose of committing a crime.
Example: *"The detective suspected an inside man was responsible for the theft, as only someone with inside knowledge could have pulled it off."*

Interrogation: The process of questioning a suspect or witness in order to gather information or elicit a confession.
Example: *"The detective's skilled interrogation led the suspect to confess to the crime, providing the final piece of evidence needed for a conviction."*

Jigsaw: A method of investigating crime in which detectives piece together evidence and information to build a complete picture of the crime and the perpetrator.
Example: *"The detective used a jigsaw approach to solving the case, slowly but surely putting together all the pieces of the puzzle."*

Jump the gun: To take action or make assumptions before all the facts are known.
Example: *"The detective was criticised for jumping the gun when he arrested the suspect without enough evidence."*

Jurisdiction: The legal authority of a law enforcement agency to investigate and prosecute crimes within a specific area.
Example: *"The detective was careful to stay within his jurisdiction as he conducted the investigation, avoiding any conflicts with neighbouring agencies."*

Lineup: A method of identifying a suspect in which a group of people are presented to a witness or victim for identification.
Example: *"The detective arranged for a line-up to be conducted, but the witness was unable to identify the suspect."*

Modus operandi (MO): The unique method or pattern of operation used by a criminal in committing crimes.
Example: *"The detective noticed a similarity in the MO of the recent burglaries and believed they were committed by the same perpetrator."*

Motive: The reason or incentive behind a crime.
Example: *"The detective uncovered a financial motive for the murder, as the victim was in possession of a large inheritance."*

Noir: A genre of crime fiction characterised by its dark, cynical tone and focus on the seedier side of society.

Example: *"The noir novel explored the gritty underbelly of the city, where corruption and vice were commonplace."*

Noir-fiction: A type of crime fiction characterised by its focus on the criminal, rather than the detective.
Example: *"The Noir fiction novel followed the inner workings of the criminal mind, and how it led to the commission of the crime."*

Noir-ish: A type of crime fiction characterised by its noir-like themes, but with a more modern and contemporary setting.
Example: *"The Noir-ish novel explored the dark side of the city and the struggles of the characters caught in it, but also showed the progress made in recent times in terms of technology and society."*

Off the books: Illegal or unethical activities that are not officially recorded or acknowledged.
Example: *"The detective uncovered a series of off the books transactions that were funding the criminal organisation."*

Parole: A conditional release from prison before the end of a sentence, usually granted to prisoners who have shown good behaviour.
Example: *"The suspect was on parole at the time of the crime, making it easy for the detective to track him down."*

Perp: Short for perpetrator, a person who has committed a crime.
Example: *"The detective was determined to catch the perp and bring him to justice."*

Plant: To place false evidence or information at a crime scene in order to mislead investigators.
Example: *"The detective suspected that the incriminating evidence found on the suspect was planted by the real perpetrator."*

Profile: A psychological or behavioural analysis of a criminal, often used to aid in the investigation and identification of suspects.

Example: *"The detective used the criminal profile to narrow down the list of suspects and focus on the most likely perpetrator."*

Racket: An illegal or unethical business or scheme.
Example: *"The detective uncovered a racket involving the sale of stolen goods and illegal weapons."*

Rap sheet: A record of a person's criminal history.
Example: *"The suspect's rap sheet showed a long history of criminal activity, making him the prime suspect in the case."*

Rat: An informer or traitor within a criminal organisation.
Example: *"The detective relied on a rat within the gang to provide him with information on their illegal activities."*

Red herring: A false clue or piece of information that leads investigators away from the truth.
Example: *"The detective suspected that the red herring of the missing watch was planted to throw him off the trail."*

Runner: A person who carries messages or delivers goods for a criminal organisation.
Example: *"The detective followed the runner, hoping to find clues to the whereabouts of the gang's leader."*

Shill: A person who pretends to be a customer in order to lend credibility to a criminal enterprise.
Example: *"The detective discovered that one of the gamblers at the illegal casino was a shill, working for the organiser of the operation."*

Snitch: Informant who gives information to the authorities or law enforcement.
Example: *"The detective was able to track down the criminal organisation thanks to the help of a snitch from within the group."*

Squeal: To inform on someone, especially a criminal.

Example: *"The suspect squealed on his accomplices in exchange for a reduced sentence."*

Stool pigeon: An informer, especially one who is used regularly by the police.
Example: *"The detective used a stool pigeon to infiltrate the criminal organisation and gather information."*

Tail: To follow or keep surveillance on someone.
Example: *"The detective tailed the suspect, hoping to gather enough evidence to make an arrest."*

Undercover: An operation or investigation in which a law enforcement officer poses as someone else in order to gather information or evidence.
Example: *"The detective went undercover, posing as a wealthy businessman to infiltrate the criminal organisation."*

Whodunit: A type of crime fiction that focuses on the process of solving a crime, rather than the crime itself.
Example: *"The whodunit novel kept readers guessing until the very end, when the true killer was finally revealed."*

Afterword

In conclusion, we hope that **"Crime 101: A Guide to Writing the Perfect Crime Novel"** has provided you with valuable insights and tips on how to create a successful crime novel.

By following the recommendations and key elements outlined in this guide, you will be able to write a novel that is both engaging and thrilling for your readers. You now have the tools to avoid common mistakes, build a compelling plot, create memorable characters, and craft engaging dialogue.

You have also learned about the importance of researching your novel, creating an opening scene that grabs your readers' attention, and how to use plot twists, red herrings, and endings to keep your readers guessing.

Additionally, you have been provided with tips on how to market your novel, create a book cover that stands out, and how to use point of view to enhance your storytelling. You now also have a writing checklist, advice on how to alleviate common fears, how to use show not tell, and how to find the right editor for your needs.

If you are ready to put everything you've learned into action, we highly recommend our companion guide **"How to Write a Winning Fiction Book Outline - Crime."**

With **done-for-you templates** and step-by-step guidance, this workbook will take everything you've learned in Crime Writing 101 and help you turn it into a compelling and exciting crime novel.

Not only will it guide you through the writing process, but it will also help you craft an irresistible plot, create unforgettable characters, and craft jaw-dropping endings and killer plot twists with ease.

We've made every step fun and the possibilities endless! And when it's time to publish, we've got you covered there too with a winning strategy for creating an eye-catching book cover, sizzling blurb, and professional sounding synopsis. So why wait?

Take the next step in your writing journey and order our companion workbook NOW!

Made in United States
Orlando, FL
22 January 2025